CAREERS *in Your Community*™

# WORKING *as a* MECHANIC *in* YOUR COMMUNITY

Mary-Lane Kamberg

ROSEN
PUBLISHING®

New York

*For Ken, my friend in the car business*

Published in 2016 by The Rosen Publishing Group, Inc.
29 East 21st Street, New York, NY 10010

Copyright © 2016 by The Rosen Publishing Group, Inc.

First Edition

**Library of Congress Cataloging-in-Publication Data**

Kamberg, Mary-Lane, 1948– author.
Working as a mechanic in your community Mary-Lane Kamberg.—First edition.
        pages cm.—(Careers in your community)
Includes bibliographical references and index.
ISBN 978-1-4994-6113-8 (library bound)
1. Automobile mechanics—Juvenile literature. 2. Automobiles—
Maintenance and repair—Vocational guidance–Juvenile literature. I. Title.
HD8039.M34K36 2016
629.28'7—dc23

                                                    2014047232

*Manufactured in the United States of America*

# Contents

4   *Introduction*

**CHAPTER** *One*
7   **A Dirty, Rewarding Job**

**CHAPTER** *Two*
18   **Start Your Engines**

**CHAPTER** *Three*
31   **Getting the Job**

**CHAPTER** *Four*
42   **Passing Lanes**

**CHAPTER** *Five*
54   **Down the Road**

67 **Glossary**
69 **For More Information**
72 **For Further Reading**
74 **Bibliography**
77 **Index**

# Introduction

**W**hy won't this car start? That's the question a master mechanic faced one day at work in a car dealer's service department. The car had a diesel engine, and even though he was certified to work as a mechanic for all types of auto maintenance and repair, he had little experience with diesel engines.

He had to figure out the problem—and it took all day. He spent nearly eight hours studying his workshop manual and running tests on various circuits and electrical components. The car had many different sensors, but he didn't know which ones went into play when trying to start the vehicle. He had codes for an open exhaust gas temperature sensor, but he didn't know if that affected starting. If the car started in the wrong conditions, this sensor makes sure the exhaust pipe doesn't get too hot and melt.

The mechanic turned back to the electrical system section of the manual. There, in the fine print, he found the answer. He learned that if he unplugged the exhaust gas temperature sensor, the car would be disabled as a safety feature. However, the sensor was still plugged in. He knew that if the electrical system on this exhaust gas temperature circuit was open, it was the same thing as being unplugged. An open circuit is a path for electric current that has been interrupted. He found the open circuit and closed it. The car started.

A day in the life of a mechanic, also called an automotive service technician, is full of surprises. Unless he or she specializes in one type of service or repair, the jobs vary from day to day. The day after working on one car for eight hours, for example, the same mechanic worked on a different car's brakes. Then he diagnosed a problem with an intermittent fog

Some automotive service technicians specialize in one kind of maintenance or repair on cars and light trucks. Others perform a wide variety of tasks.

light on a truck, replaced a gas tank part that had been recalled for another truck, reprogrammed computer modules on four different cars, worked on a clutch on another (but had to wait to finish it until the right part arrived), diagnosed and fixed an overheating condition on an SUV engine, and diagnosed and fixed a transmission shift problem on another car.

Automotive service technicians make important contributions to their community. First, they keep streets safer by ensuring the cars driving on them operate correctly. Second, some of their work keeps down emissions that can be harmful to the environment. Third, they save residents money by finding problems early when repairs are less expensive and by enabling car owners to repair their vehicles instead of having to replace them.

If you're interested in serving your community this way, it's easy to find out what the job involves, what skills you need, how to prepare for the career, where to find training, how to find job openings, and the future outlook for men and women in the field. Read on to see if a career as an automotive service technician is one that suits you.

# CHAPTER One

# A Dirty, Rewarding Job

Not every community needs an aerospace engineer, printing press operator, or surfboard manufacturer. But even a small town needs at least one person— and usually many more—who knows how to maintain and repair motor vehicles. The work of an automotive service technician is vital to the well-being of everyone who drives.

These skilled technicians inspect, maintain, and repair cars and light trucks. A light truck or light-duty truck is an American designation for a vehicle that weighs up to 14,000 pounds (6,350 kilograms) with a payload capacity of less than 4,000 pounds (1,815 kg). Examples of light trucks include the Chevrolet Silverado 2500, Dodge Dakota, Dodge Ram 2500, Dodge Ram 3500, Ford F-250, Ford F-350, GMC Canyon, GMC Sierra 3500, Hummer H1, and Toyota Tacoma.

# Up and Down and Dirty

Mechanics work under the hood, as well as under the car itself—either on their backs on the ground or standing under a lift, a machine that raises the car off the floor. They are also found crawling around the inside of the vehicle to check sensors or make repairs, sometimes in uncomfortable positions. Working as a mechanic requires them to get their hands and clothes dirty. Grease, oil, and other fluids often find their way to the mechanic's skin and clothes. Many wear aprons or other protective clothing during their shifts.

A mechanic's workplace may be an open-air garage with no heat or air conditioning. However, most

As is the case with many repairs that mechanics make, working on a motor vehicle's transmission is a get-your-hands-and-clothes-dirty task. Many mechanics wear aprons to protect their clothes or uniforms.

mechanics today work in well-ventilated and well-lit repair shops. Most of them work full time, and many work evenings and/or weekends. Paid overtime is common.

# WHERE AUTOMOTIVE SERVICE TECHNICIANS WORK

Auto mechanics work in a wide variety of environments. According to the U.S. Department of Labor's most recent survey in 2012, most auto technicians worked in repair and maintenance businesses and automobile dealerships. Here are the percentages of these workers who worked in each type of place:

- *Automotive repair and maintenance*          *32%*
- *Automobile dealers*                          *29%*
- *Automotive parts, accessories, and tire stores*  *9%*
- *Governments (federal, state, and local)*     *4%*
- *Gasoline stations*                           *3%*

Service technicians get paid hourly or by the job. Experienced mechanics at many dealerships and independent repair shops get commissions for the work they perform. A commission is a fee based on a percentage of money the employer receives from a customer. Other employers pay fixed hourly rates. Some pay systems are determined by negotiated union contracts.

In some places, mechanics are paid by the job according to a certain amount of time it should take to finish the task. For example, a job mounting and balancing four tires might pay 1.6 hours, whether the mechanic takes twenty minutes or all week to do it. If he or she is good enough to finish the job correctly in under 1.6 hours, the pay is still the mechanic's hourly pay rate times 1.6. Therefore, it pays to be efficient. Under this type of arrangement, for example, a mechanic might work for eight hours and get paid for twelve hours because he or she worked fast enough to complete the jobs in less time. Taking too long or making a mistake and having to do a job over pays nothing extra. The system can frustrate a technician who has trouble getting a component to come apart easily or who must redo work a customer (or less qualified mechanic) tried on his or her own. A particular job that should take only an hour may take two or three hours, but the technician gets no extra pay.

A mechanic's job is relatively safe when safety procedures are followed. For instance, a mechanic may wear goggles to protect the eyes from flying metal scrapings or special mechanics' gloves to prevent burns from acid or a hot exhaust pipe. However, minor workplace injuries such as cuts, sprains, and bruises are common. Still, mechanics enjoy a sense of independence as they work. They also like the mental challenge of figuring out problems.

Employers evaluate mechanics by how many jobs they can do in a day—and how well they do them. Bosses also look at the number of "comebacks" the mechanic is responsible for. A comeback is a customer who returns with a car that was not fixed during the first visit. Too many comebacks, and the mechanic is asked not to come back!

# Hey! Look Me Over!

Automotive technicians often inspect cars for customers who want a heads-up about their car's condition or who must satisfy conditions of the car's warranty. During a routine service inspection, technicians follow a checklist that includes belts, hoses, plugs, and brake and fuel systems. They test and lubricate engines. If they find worn parts, they recommend repair or replacement to the owner.

In some areas, technicians also inspect vehicles according to state and local laws governing safety and the environment. The technician checks such vehicle parts as the lights, horn, and windshield wipers. The Missouri vehicle safety inspection program, for

In addition to repairing broken parts, mechanics also inspect vehicles for safety and maintenance issues. Owners can then take care of potential problems before their vehicle breaks.

example, is regulated by the State Highway Patrol. The program's purpose is to ensure that no vehicle poses a threat to the driver, passengers, or other drivers on the road, and that it complies with Missouri safety laws.

In areas where required, inspectors also check the chemical quality of a car's or truck's emissions, the gases released as waste products of the engine. Some states, such as New York, Illinois, and Nevada, require vehicles to pass smog and emissions tests. Others have no statewide testing requirement, but there may be exceptions in certain areas with more air

# IS YOUR FAMILY CAR SAFE TO DRIVE?

Many states require that vehicles pass safety inspections before they can be registered and licensed. Automotive service technicians and others with special training perform these tests. In Missouri, for example, the following parts must be in good working order:

- *Seat belts*
- *Windshield and windows*
- *Turn signals and headlights*
- *Brake lights*
- *Brake system*
- *Horn*
- *Steering mechanism*
- *Rearview mirrors*
- *Exhaust system*
- *Fuel system*
- *Tires and wheels*
- *Bumpers*
- *Airbags*

pollution. For example, in Oregon, most vehicles in the Portland and Medford metropolitan areas must pass a Department of Environmental Quality emissions test as part of the registration tag renewal process. According to the Oregon Department of Motor Vehicles, motorized vehicles are the state's number-one source of air pollution. The department's website says, "Emissions lead to high smog and carbon monoxide levels, which can have a variety of effects on Oregonians."

# Tender Loving Care

Service technicians also perform maintenance tasks that keep a car or truck in good condition before something breaks. Examples of maintenance jobs include changing the oil, replacing oil and air filters, replacing fluids, rotating tires (changing the placement of each tire to ensure even wear), and replacing brake pads, wheel bearings, batteries, and tires. Performing maintenance tasks requires no diagnostic skills.

These jobs usually go to "journeymen" or "journeywomen," mechanics who have served an apprenticeship at a trade school or working under a more experienced mechanic. They are certified to work as mechanics, but they may have little hands-on experience. Maintenance tasks include fewer parts than those required for major repair work. Working on these types of jobs helps the mechanics become familiar with the different systems that make a vehicle run.

A mechanic's job may also include fixing or replacing parts because of a factory recall. A factory recall occurs when a specific part on a number of cars breaks often or when a part creates a safety issue. In late 2014, for example, Volkswagen recalled 400,602 Jetta models

Mechanics who work in dealerships often replace parts because of manufacturer recalls. In 2014, for example, Volkswagen recalled Beetles and Beetle convertibles to ensure the safety of the rear-suspension system.

manufactured between 2011 and 2013 and 41,663 Beetle and Beetle Convertible models produced between 2012 and 2013, according to the *Wall Street Journal*. The recall required inspection of the rear suspension system. At issue was a part called the rear trailing arm. The arm connects the rear axle to the body of the car. Volkswagen learned that a rear-end collision could weaken the part. If the driver failed to repair it, the part could suddenly break and cause another accident.

The same week as the Volkswagen recall, another car manufacturer issued its own safety recalls. Toyota recalled 1.67 million vehicles to check a range of problems from faulty brakes to fuel line parts, again according to the *Wall Street Journal*. Mechanics who are called on to replace parts involved in a recall gain a lot of experience in a short time because they replace the same part again and again. However, some dealerships pay less for replacing parts for recalls than for other repairs.

The same may hold true for repairs "under factory warranty." A factory warranty is a written guarantee that a manufacturer issues to a car buyer. It promises to repair or replace the car, if necessary, within a specified period of time. Dealerships often pay mechanics less for doing such repairs.

# Where Does It Hurt?

Like a medical doctor diagnosing a sick patient, ser-vice technicians must diagnose what is wrong with a car that a customer brings in for repair. The investiga-tion begins by listening to the customer's description of the problem. Technicians ask such questions as:

- *What "symptoms" did the owner notice?*
- *Did the car make unusual noises?*
- *Where do the noises seem to come from?*
- *What was the car doing when the problem appeared? (Stopping? Turning? Starting? Going uphill?)*
- *When did the customer first notice the problem?*
- *Does the problem happen all the time or come and go?*

Once the automotive service technician figures out what's wrong with a vehicle brought in for repair, he or she may show the customer the parts that need to be replaced.

The answers are the first clues in solving the mystery of what's wrong and what repairs are likely needed. Sometimes the service technician drives the car to see if he or she can make the car do what the customer describes.

The next step is using specialized diagnostic testing equipment to check computerized sensors built into the car. Modern cars have five or more computers onboard. These give the technician readings that help diagnose the trouble, but they don't solve the mystery. The mechanic can see which sensors' readings are not what they should be. However, coming up with the right answer is up to the mechanic, based on his or her training, experience, and problem-solving skills.

The mechanic might test parts and systems to see if they're working properly or take apart components of the car and put them back together. Once the cause of the issue is found, the technician estimates the cost of parts and labor to fix the car. In some shops, mechanics deal directly with the customer. In others, workers called service advisers deal with customer communication. They explain the problem, give the customer options, and discuss the cost of the repair and potential future repairs.

If the customer approves the estimate, the technician, service adviser, or some other employee orders the necessary parts. Sometimes waiting for parts to arrive means the mechanic must temporarily stop working on the car. In the meantime, he or she will start work on a different car.

# CHAPTER *Two*

# Start Your Engines

Automotive service technicians need a wide variety of personal and professional skills, as well as certification and, in some cases, licensing. Technicians work with their hands, so they need dexterity, good hand-eye coordination, and the ability to use hand tools. They also need the strength to lift heavy tools and parts.

Apart from physical traits, future mechanics should enjoy taking things apart and putting them back together. Being systematic, logical, and detail oriented are other important qualities when inspecting, diagnosing, and repairing vehicles.

Potential technicians must have earned a high school diploma or Certificate of High School Equivalency by passing the General Educational Development (GED) test. The GED test includes science, mathematics, social studies, reading, and writing.

Along with technical knowledge, mechanics need courtesy and good manners. They must work well with others, especially their customers and coworkers.

Service technicians must be responsible and dependable. (So must workers in any field of employment.) They also need personal traits such as patience, courtesy, and good communication skills. Patience wards off frustration when problems are hard to solve. It also helps when repairs become difficult, such as when a mechanic can't seem to get a part to come off. Good manners are important in any line of work dealing with others, whether coworkers or customers. And explaining complicated engineering concepts to customers in easy-to-understand ways takes good communication skills.

## You Have a Lot to Learn

If you have those physical and personal qualities and want to become an automotive service technician, the next most important skill is the ability to use computers and computerized equipment. Automobile and light truck technology heavily depends on computer skills, including programming. Troubleshooting depends on diagnostic equipment for engine systems and components of mechanical and electronic systems that are becoming more and more complex. As car and light truck manufacturing evolves, service technicians also need to adapt to new computer-based technology.

Future mechanics also need specific knowledge about cars and light trucks. That means knowing engine components and electronic control systems and understanding how they work together. A strong background in tinkering with one's own car helps. So does knowing the engineering concepts that apply. Service technicians also need familiarity with all the tools used to fix and maintain vehicles.

Fortunately, you can find places to learn what you need to know right in your own community. Take classes in high school in automotive repair, electronics, computers, mathematics, physics, and English. Try your school or local public library for how-to books, videos, and other resources. Search the Internet for more help. For example, a Google search for "how to change oil on a car" yields more than six million websites with everything you need to know for that one task.

If possible, ask someone in the automotive or other motor repair business if you can spend time in a garage

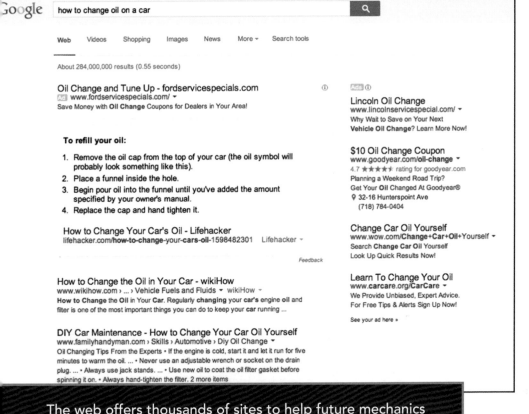

The web offers thousands of sites to help future mechanics learn about the systems that work together to make a car or light truck run properly.

or repair shop observing a trained technician at work. You might pursue a hobby or take classes that teach you how to work on small motors. Look for weekend workshops offered by local businesses and noncredit community college classes in related topics such as lawn mower repair and motorcycle maintenance. The Johnson County Community College in Overland Park, Kansas, for example, offers a twelve-hour motorcycle maintenance course that covers basic maintenance, safety inspection, ignition systems, electrical circuits, steering, and other fundamentals.

Clubs and other organizations offer special interest programs about automotive topics. For example, the Girl Scouts of the USA, with the help of Firestone Complete Auto Care™ and the U.S. Department of Labor, developed an interactive resource guide called On the Road. The guide includes safe driving tips, basic vehicle maintenance, and a list of career opportunities in the automotive industry.

The Boy Scouts of America award an automotive maintenance merit badge. Members who complete the requirements for it learn about the functions of most vehicle systems and gain skills in the following areas:

- *Safety issues when working on cars*
- *Checking levels of oil, brake fluid, coolant, and*

The Boy Scouts of America offer a merit badge in automotive maintenance. Requirements include learning about safety issues, vehicle power systems, and how to change oil and check tire pressure.

*power steering, windshield washer, and transmission fluids*
- *Replacing fuses*
- *Checking belts, hoses, and air filters*
- *Understanding dashboard lights, symbols, and gauges*
- *Checking tire pressure and inflating tires*
- *Differences among internal combustion, diesel, and hybrid vehicle power systems*
- *Flushing and changing engine coolant*
- *Understanding automatic and manual transmissions*
- *Understanding the differences between front-wheel, rear-wheel, and four-wheel drive*
- *Understanding the difference between disc and drum brake systems and how to check for wear*
- *Learning about career opportunities in the automotive industry*

# Training Days

So, how do you get the training you need? Look in your own community. Most areas have nearby private vocational/technical schools or community colleges for formal training in the field. Programs at private technical schools usually take between six and eighteen months to complete. If you can't find one close to home, look for online or distance learning mechanic schools offered by schools such as Ashworth College, Penn Foster Schools, Stratford Career Institute, and Universal Technical Institute (UTI).

Many community colleges offer two-year associate's degrees in automotive service that also include courses in basic mathematics, computers,

Many formal training programs for mechanics in vocational schools and community colleges include hands-on experience under the guidance of a trained professional.

electronics, customer service, English, and general engineering topics such as how fuel systems work. These degree programs also include hands-on experience with real vehicles and up-to-date diagnostic equipment.

Automobile manufacturers and dealers also sponsor associate's degree programs. Students in these programs alternate classroom work with real-world experience, learning maintenance and repair from experienced mechanics. Instead of generic engineering topics, these factory schools teach about their own models. For example, the Ford Motor Company program covers the fuel systems (and other systems) on the Ford Fusion and/or Ford Escape.

The Ford Automotive Student Service Educational Training (ASSET) program operates at eighty-eight locations in the United States. It works in partnership with local dealerships and community colleges. Students must work for and be sponsored by a Ford or Lincoln dealer. It's an associate's degree program with a paid internship. Over the two-year period, students earn while they learn, alternating six to eight weeks in the classroom with six to eight weeks working at the sponsoring dealership.

The Ford Accelerated Credential Training (FACT) program is a fifteen-week certificate program that partners with UTI. Students may enroll in FACT after completing a one-year core program. FACT training includes Ford-specific instruction for their Quick Lane Tire and Auto Center®, as well as vehicle inspections and other topics. Upon completion, students get job placement support.

Ford also offers a one-year certificate program that qualifies students to go right to work in maintenance and light repair. Factory-trained instructors at community colleges teach the course. In addition, Ford offers a one-year Youth and Adult Automotive Training Center certificate program that includes job readiness and life skills topics, as well as automotive technology.

# THE FORD/AAA STUDENT AUTO SKILLS COMPETITION

The Ford Motor Company cosponsors an annual nationwide competition for automotive service students who are high school juniors or seniors. In 2013, students won a total of $11 million in scholarships and prizes.

Ford's cosponsor, AAA (pronounced "Triple A"), is a nonprofit federation of motor clubs with fifty-four million members in the United States and Canada. The organization offers services such as roadside assistance, insurance, trip planning, safety education, and approvals of high-quality auto repair facilities. Together these sponsors hope to promote interest in automotive technology careers among young people.

Teams of two to five high school students take an online written exam. Those who qualify at the state level compete in a hands-on contest to diagnose and fix a "bugged" vehicle with the highest-quality workmanship in the shortest time. All vehicles have been bugged the same way. State winners get paid travel and luxury hotel accommodations for the

Founded in 1902, AAA continues to promote good roads and safety education, as well as provide roadside assistance and other services for motorists.

national competition in Dearborn, Michigan, at the Ford Motor Company headquarters.

Prizes vary slightly year to year, but teams usually compete for scholarships, trophies, apparel, tools, trips, and automotive equipment for their schools. The 2014 grand prize was a once-in-a-lifetime job shadow with Wood Brothers Racing. The winning team worked alongside top automotive technicians on actual race cars, attended a race in VIP style, and more!

# Showing Your Creds

Most employers prefer—and some require—mechanics to have earned certification in the trade. Certification from the National Institute for Automotive Service Excellence (ASE) is the standard credential they look for. To earn the certificate, the aspiring service technician needs two years of hands-on experience. Work in a formal automotive training program may satisfy this requirement.

In addition, the aspiring mechanic must pass one or more certification exams. Each certification allows the mechanic to perform tasks in that area. Someone who qualifies in all eight areas becomes certified as a master automotive technician. A master technician, also called a master tech or master mechanic, can work on every system on a vehicle.

Tests are available in eight subject areas:

- *Engine repair*
- *Automatic transmission/transaxle*
- *Manual drive train and axles*
- *Suspension and steering*
- *Brakes*
- *Electrical/electronic systems*
- *Heating and air conditioning*
- *Engine performance*

Technicians qualified in only one or a few areas become proficient because they perform the same task over and over. They can often complete more jobs in less time than a master can, thus making more money for that job than the more qualified technician.

However, the master mechanic has more opportunities to take jobs since he or she can work on anything that comes into the shop. For example, if the shop gets a high volume of one type of repair, such as transmission work, the master technician can back up the specialized technician in much the same way a utility infielder in baseball can play any base, plus shortstop. A master technician is a valuable employee because he or she can back up every specialized technician in the service department.

# A LOOK AT THE ASE CERTIFICATION EXAM

Before taking the ASE exam, it's a good idea to practice with a manual of sample tests. Here are some examples of test questions on various ASE tests from *Automotive Technician Certification Test Preparation Manual* (4th edition), by Don Knowles and Bob Rodriguez:

**1.** An engine has a clattering noise when the engine is accelerated and decelerated. The most likely cause of this problem is:
   a. worn main bearings.
   b. loose connecting rod bearings.
   c. sticking valve lifters.
   d. worn push rods.

*(continued on the next page)*

*(continued from the previous page)*

**2.** The fluid in an automatic transaxle is a dark brown color and smells burned. Technician A says this problem may be caused by a worn front planetary sun gear. Technician B says this problem may be caused by worn friction-type clutch plates. Who is correct?

    a. A only
    b. B only
    c. Both A and B
    d. Neither A nor B

**3.** A front-wheel drive car has a clicking noise while cornering at low speeds. The most likely cause of this problem is a(n):

    a. worn outer CV joint.
    b. worn wheel bearing.
    c. worn inner CV joint.
    d. out-of-balance wheel.

Answers:　1. b; 2. a; 3. a.

In addition to ASE certifications, technicians who work on motor vehicle air conditioning systems must be licensed to handle refrigerants. These licenses are required by Section 609 of the Clean Air Act, Motor Vehicle Air Conditioning. Applicants must pass the Environmental Protection Agency's (EPA's) licensing exam. Many trade schools, unions, and employer associations offer training programs to prepare students for the EPA exam.

# CHAPTER *Three*

# Getting the Job

Jake Temple was a junior in business school at the University of Kansas when his 250cc Honda Rebel motorcycle broke down. He couldn't fix it himself. He came from a family with little mechanical aptitude. He didn't even know what a $7/8$ wrench was. (A wrench is a common hand tool used for holding, turning, or twisting automotive parts and other items; $7/8$-inch is a wrench size.) He took his motorcycle to a repair shop.

"They had my bike for four months and couldn't fix it," Temple said. "But I thought it couldn't be that hard."

He took a class in motorcycle maintenance and repair at a community college near home. He found that he liked learning how to fix his bike and working with his hands. He left the University of Kansas and enrolled in a two-year program at the same community college. He earned an associate's degree in automotive technology.

Six months later, he got a job as a lube technician at a Ford dealership in Overland Park, Kansas. He changed oil, mounted tires, and replaced batteries for three and a half years. He also worked to earn

Hands-on experience is an essential qualification for those who hope to become mechanics. Along with certifications and licenses, practice helps them perform tasks efficiently.

certification as a master mechanic. The dealer sent him to a Ford factory school, where he learned about Ford models.

Like Temple, most new service technicians must complete on-the-job training. To become fully qualified takes two to five years. Becoming familiar with all types of automotive repairs takes another year or two. New technicians start at the internship or entry level. They start as trainee technicians, technicians' helpers, or lubrication workers.

"A degree alone is not enough," Temple said. "If you have no experience, you're going to be changing oil."

Still, Temple values his education. He said it gave him a solid foundation in the engineering that goes into a car's design. "Guys who grew up fixing cars can repair things," he said. "But they may know only the basics, not the minute engineering. If you have that, you'll be one of the best."

## Tools of the Trade

Along with education, certification, licensing, and experience, mechanics also need tools. And while their employers usually own computerized diagnostic tools and power tools such as lathes, welding torches, jacks, and hoists, mechanics typically own their own hand tools. They need hand wrenches, pliers, sockets, ratchets, and both slotted (flat-blade) and Phillips screwdrivers in a variety of sizes. For most cars today, mechanics use metric tools, but they may also need standard tools for vehicles built according to the imperial system of measurement. Some mechanics also own impact wrenches powered by compressed air.

If they get a job they don't have the right tool for, they have to go buy it. Mechanics sometimes borrow tools, but it's not typical. "If you're super good friends with the other mechanic, it's not a problem," Temple said. "If you don't know the other guy that well, you won't even ask."

In 2014 alone, Temple estimated he spent $10,000 on tools. "Over a lifetime, a mechanic can have $100,000 invested in tools," he said. Tools aren't cheap, but Temple recommends getting high-quality ones. "They're more expensive, but they have a lifetime warranty," he said. "Cheaper ones won't last."

# Start Spreading the Word

Once you're qualified for a job as an automotive service technician, start by creating a one-page résumé. Put your name and contact information at the top of the page. Then add a brief sentence about your career goals. For example: "Objective: To work in an entry-level position as a trainee technician, with a long-term goal of becoming an automotive service technician specializing in engine performance."

Include sections about your education, training, and any employment experience. List clubs or other activities that relate to the industry. If you are a NASCAR season-ticket holder or race motorcycles, put it down. If you like fly fishing, leave it out. Also omit age, marital status, family information, ethnic background, and religious and political beliefs. If a potential employer asks for references, put them on a separate piece of paper, not on the résumé itself.

Next, tell everyone you know that you're looking for a job as a mechanic. Many workers, no matter what their field, got their jobs through personal contacts. Ask if anyone knows someone in the auto service industry. Ask them to help you connect with someone in the business. Or contact local auto dealers and repair shops yourself. Make a list of names and contact information.

Using your list, try to find a technician to talk to as an informational interview. An informational interview is a conversation with a professional to learn about the field and local job market. Ask for an appointment for a fifteen-minute interview.

Make a list of questions to ask. Some typical questions include:

- *How did you become a mechanic?*
- *What do you like best and least about the job?*
- *What tips do you have for someone starting out?*
- *What is the range of salaries in the community?*
- *Do you know of any positions open right now?*

Conduct the interview in person. Arrive on time and stay only as long as the agreed time limit. Thank the technician. Leave your name and contact information in case the technician later learns of a job opening you might be a good fit for. Send a thank-you e-mail or handwritten thank-you note. From time to time, drop the mechanic a note or e-mail to stay in touch. When you land a job, let him or her know where you are working and again give thanks for the help.

# Where to Find Jobs

Look for job listings you're qualified for. If you've earned a certificate or graduated from a vocational school or community college, you may get job placement assistance there. Check with your teachers or advisor. Search Internet job sites for openings in your area. Or enter "job openings auto service" and your city and state into your web browser.

In some areas, automotive service technicians belong to labor unions such as the International Union, United Automobile, Aerospace and

# WEBSITES FOR JOB HUNTERS

When you're ready to look for a job as an automotive service technician, search reputable job websites such as these. Many let you include your ZIP code or city and state in the search box to help you find work in your own community.

The Internet offers a variety of job-search tools, including websites that list job openings and information about unions that serve mechanics in your community.

- CareerBuilder.com
- Craigslist.org
- JobsMonster.com
- Jobs.net
- NeedTechs.com
- TopUSAJobs.com
- Auto-technicians.jobs.net
- Indeed.com
- Snagajob.com
- Unionjobs.com

Agricultural Implement Workers of America (UAW), one of the largest unions in the United States. Other unions that include mechanics are the International Association of Machinists and Aerospace Workers, the Sheet Metal Workers' International Association, and the International Brotherhood of Teamsters. Find out whether mechanics in your community belong to unions by searching the union websites for lists of union shops in your area. Add the employers to your job search list. You can also use online union job banks. Finally, attend labor council meetings near you. (They're open to the public.) Meet technicians who are union members, and ask about job openings in union shops.

You can join a union only if you work for a business that has a labor contract with a union. A labor contract is an agreement between the employer and its employees. It results from negotiations between employers and the union. If you get a job at such a business, you'll be covered by the agreement. In some states, workers must join the appropriate union and pay dues as a condition of employment. In twenty-four other states, employees have the "right to work" without joining a union. In those states, mostly in the South and Midwest, unions represent all employees whether they join the union or not.

According to the National Right to Work Legal Defense Foundation, in 2014 the following twenty-four states had right-to-work laws: Alabama, Arizona, Arkansas, Florida, Georgia, Guam, Idaho, Indiana, Iowa, Kansas, Louisiana, Michigan, Mississippi, Nevada, North Carolina, North Dakota, Oklahoma, South Carolina, South Dakota, Tennessee, Texas, Utah, Virginia, and Wyoming. In addition, the state of Colorado had a law with right-to-work provisions, but it also allowed union-only employers if employees wanted a closed union shop.

## Talk to Me

Narrow your job search to places you'd like to work. Then contact the businesses and ask for an application and job interview. A job interview is a conversation between an employer and a potential employee. The employer's goal is to find a new worker. The potential employee's goal is to get a job offer. If your first contact is by telephone, try to calm any nerves you have. Speak slowly and clearly, and keep a confident tone in your voice.

After you get an interview appointment, prepare for it. Learn as much as you can about the employer. Check its website. Search for news

Be sure to fill out formal applications neatly and check your spelling. Next, prepare for an interview by learning all you can about the employer.

articles about the business and its owners. Ask others in the community what they know about it. Does it have a good reputation with customers and past or present workers? How long has it been in business? Also check the Internet for information about the person who will interview you. Enter the interviewer's name in your web browser. Look on social media sites. What do you have in common with the person?

Practice interview skills with a parent or friend. Being a little nervous is normal. Make a list of possible questions the interviewer might ask. Good examples include:

- *Why do you want this type of work?*
- *How can you contribute to this business?*
- *What types of maintenance and repair jobs do you like best?*
- *What is your training and work experience?*
- *What are your long-term goals in this industry?*

Be ready with brief, simple, and specific answers. You'll build confidence with a few rehearsals. But don't memorize answers or practice too much. Your actual interview should be easy and natural.

Eye contact and a friendly smile go a long way during a job interview. Even if you feel a bit nervous, try to come across as confident in your training and abilities.

Dress for the job you want. Automotive technicians usually wear uniforms, so you don't need a suit and tie or business-appropriate dress. Instead, wear something such as a shirt with a collar and khaki pants. Avoid T-shirts or jeans. Be sure your hair—including facial hair—is clean and neat.

The day of the interview, plan ahead. Try to arrive between five and ten minutes before the appointment. Allow yourself plenty of travel time, as well as about fifteen minutes extra to allow for mini emergencies en route. Turn off your mobile phone before entering the place of work.

During the interview, stay calm. Start in a friendly, confident way, but try not to seem cocky. Smile and use a firm handshake. Look the interviewer in the eye. Listen carefully to the questions. Keep in mind that the more you let the interviewer talk, the more he or she will like you!

Ask your own questions. What duties would you perform at first? What opportunities will there be for you to learn more and gain more experience? Avoid questions about benefits or vacations. Focus on what you can do for the business. Ask how soon the employer will make a decision. At the end of the interview, smile and shake hands again. Express interest in getting the job. Check back in a few days via phone, e-mail, or handwritten thank-you note. If you get a job offer, ask about hours and pay rates, along with any other benefits. If you want the job, take it!

# CHAPTER *Four*

# Passing Lanes

Getting ahead in an automotive service career depends on what success means to you. Does it mean making more money? Working on your favorite tasks? Owning your own shop?

Service technicians working for the top five types of automotive businesses earn the most money, starting with local, state, and federal governments. Those employed by automobile dealers made the next highest wages. Coming in third, fourth, and fifth, with about the same average pay, are automotive repair and maintenance businesses; parts, accessories, and tire stores; and gasoline stations. The U.S. Department of Labor's Bureau of Labor Statistics keeps records on how much workers earn in different fields. Visit the agency's website (www.bls.gov) for the most current figures on automotive service careers.

Today, the work of automotive service technicians has evolved from mechanical repair to a high-tech career. Electronic systems and complex computers in cars and light trucks require these workers to gain a broad foundation about how these components work

Mechanics can deposit higher paychecks as they gain experience in a specific area or complete additional formal training in factory or vocational schools.

and how they work together. Electronic diagnostic equipment and computer-based technical reference materials need operators who not only easily work with this technology but who can also adapt as manufacturers introduce new technology and new tools.

Getting experience working with today's vehicles is an important way to increase your income. So is continuing education through vocational or manufacturer's schools as new technology hits the market. The ability to work on more types of tasks can also lead to earning more money. Entry-level workers must "pay their dues" by working on lower-level tasks for several years before advancing to become a specialist in a particular type of work or a master mechanic who is qualified to work on all automotive systems.

# Specialization

Service technicians sometimes specialize in a particular type of repair, and some employers prefer these specialty technicians. These workers must gain an in-depth understanding of the areas they focus on, including government regulations or required procedures for the system.

## Automotive Air-Conditioning Repairers

Service techs who specialize in air-conditioning install and repair vehicle air conditioners. They also deal with compressors, condensers, and controls. Because emissions can affect Earth's ozone layer, the Clean Air Act requires mechanics to be trained in EPA regulations related to their work.

Automotive service technicians who specialize in drivability issues work on emissions systems as well as fuel, electrical, and ignition systems.

## Brake Repairers

Technicians who specialize in brakes adjust brakes and replace brake rotors and pads. Brake rotors are discs (as in "disc brakes") that brake pads push against to stop a car's wheels from spinning. Brake pads on both sides of the disc create friction that slows and stops the vehicle. Brake repairers also make other repairs on brake systems. Some brake repairers also specialize in front-end work.

## Front-End Mechanics

Front-end mechanics often use special alignment equipment and wheel-balancing machines to align and balance wheels. Wheel alignment means adjusting the wheels so they are parallel to each other and perpendicular to the ground. If a car is out of alignment, its tires wear unevenly, which reduces tire life. If wheels are properly positioned, the car will drive straight on a straight, level road without drifting to one side or the other. Some alignments involve replacement of loose or worn parts.

Wheel balancing eliminates vibrations when driving. The vibrations are caused by a wheel and tire combination that has a section that is heavier than other places. To balance the wheel, technicians place a lead weight on the wheel on the opposite side of where the heavy spot is. Front-end specialists also repair steering mechanisms and suspension systems.

## Transmission Technicians and Rebuilders

Technicians need extensive knowledge to work on both manual and automatic transmissions. A transmission uses gears to keep an engine operating at an appropriate speed. A gear is a set of toothed wheels that work together to change the relationship (ratio) between the speed of an engine and the speed of the car's tires. The main difference between the two types of transmissions concerns these gears. A manual transmission works with different sets of gears for different ratios. An automatic transmission uses one set of gears for all ratios. Transmission technicians and rebuilders need to diagnose electrical and hydraulic problems. They also work on the complex components contained in a transmission system.

Extensive knowledge of both manual and automatic transmissions is important for technicians who repair or rebuild transmission systems. Transmission technicians also diagnose electrical and hydraulic problems.

### Drivability Technicians

Drivability issues involve emission, fuel, electrical, and ignition systems that contribute to an engine's performance. These kinds of technicians use the car's onboard diagnostic system as well as electronic testing equipment such as a multimeter to find the cause of a malfunction. A multimeter is an electronic instrument that tests multiple properties of an electrical circuit, such as resistance, voltage, and current.

## Changing Lanes

If you are a qualified automotive technician but have trouble finding work or success, you might explore fields related to your occupation. Other types of mechanics need many of the same traits and skills. These occupations, which require a high school diploma or GED certificate, include automotive body and glass repairers, diesel service technicians, heavy vehicle and mobile equipment service technicians, and small engine mechanics.

If your car is involved in an accident, you'll need an automotive body and glass repairer. These technicians restore, refinish, and replace a vehicle's body or frame. They also replace broken windshields and window glass from collisions, storm damage, or other causes.

Buses, trucks, and other vehicles with diesel engines need diesel service technicians and mechanics to inspect, repair, or overhaul them. Like a gasoline engine, a diesel engine is an internal combustion engine. It changes chemical energy from fuel into mechanical energy. The mechanical energy moves pistons connected to a crankshaft, which in turn creates the circular motion that turns the wheels.

# OFF TO THE RACES

If you're interested in work as a mechanic and also like motor sports, you might become a member of a racing team in a racing series sanctioned by the National Association for Stock Car Auto Racing (NASCAR), Indy Car, or Formula One. Mechanics who join pit crews must work fast. A typical pit stop, which includes refueling and tire changes, lasts only about fifteen seconds. Pit crew members in Le Mans series racing take a little longer and may perform routine inspections

*(continued on the next page)*

Mechanics who work on pit crews in motor sports need specialized training as well as strength, agility, and speed to keep race cars ready for top performance.

(continued from the previous page)

and replace brake pads or parts of the suspension as well as the quick fix issues in other series.

The number of mechanics allowed in a pit crew varies according to the type of race. Formula One pit crews can have eighteen members, while those for Indy Cars have six. NASCAR allows seven mechanics in the pit crew, with an eighth who may join during the second half of the race. Le Mans crews have a maximum of five mechanics.

Specialized training is required for these jobs. Mechanics who work for NASCAR, for example, need complete understanding of auto engines, mechanical technology, and transmissions. They can get that knowledge through experience or a technical school. They also need a fifteen-week NASCAR-specific course in racing fundamentals, from engines, fabrication, and welding to aerodynamics and pit crew essentials. Universal Technical Institute's NASCAR Technical Institute in Mooresville, North Carolina, is the only school sponsored and endorsed by NASCAR. Some schools for other series are located in Charlotte, North Carolina.

In a gasoline engine, the fuel is mixed with air, compressed, and ignited by sparks from spark plugs. In a diesel engine, the air is compressed before the fuel enters the chamber. Heat from the compressed air ignites the fuel. Diesel fuel has a higher density than gasoline. Plus, diesel engines are more efficient than those powered by gasoline. That's why cars with diesel engines get better mileage than their gasoline counterparts.

Heavy vehicle and mobile equipment service technicians inspect, maintain, and repair vehicles and machinery used in construction, farming, railroad transportation, and other industries. Small engine mechanics inspect, service, and repair motorized power equipment in motorcycles, motorboats, or outdoor power equipment. Small engine mechanics often specialize in one type of equipment.

# Getting Down to Business

Some mechanics dream of owning their own service and repair shops. One way to do that is to start your own business. Another is to buy one that is already established. That's what Elyzabeth Goerger did. She now owns Star Fleet Services in West Fargo, North Dakota. The shop services fleet vehicles for companies such as FedEx. It also services all types of vehicles for individual customers in the community.

Goerger grew up learning about cars. Her father built hot rods, and her brother owns an auto recycling center in Minnesota. About two years before she bought the repair shop, she took her car there for repairs. She knew one of the mechanics who worked there, and he let her help work on her own car. She did such a good job that the owner hired her as a part-time light duty mechanic on weekends.

Soon she became a full-time employee. Two years later, the owner retired, and Goerger bought the business. She spends some of her marketing efforts trying to attract female customers by developing a reputation for explaining service issues to those who may not be as familiar with cars as she is. As she told *Prairie Business*, "You just have to be patient and explain."

Another way to own an automotive service is to buy a franchise from a national or international business. A franchise is a right to market a business's products or services in a specific territory. The business sells a franchise to an individual or group.

For example, Jiffy Lube International has more than two thousand fast-lube service centers in North America. They serve more than thirty million customers, according to the company's website. These centers provide preventive maintenance services such as oil changes and filter and belt replacements. The company operates some of its centers. Others are owned by franchise holders.

Jiffy Lube offers its franchisees support, service, guidance, and leadership. The company also helps

One way for a mechanic to own his or her own shop is to buy a franchise for a business such as a Jiffy Lube fast-lube service center.

the owner find a location, trains the owner and management staff, sets up an efficient operation, and provides advertising materials. In some cases, Jiffy Lube also helps qualified franchisees get financing. On its website, the company predicts that the fast-lube industry will expand over the next ten years to service more than 120 million vehicles a year, compared to about eighty million a year serviced in 1995.

Whether starting your own business or becoming a franchise holder, you'll need more than automotive service technician skills. A background or formal education in business and marketing is essential for success.

# CHAPTER Five

# Down the Road

What does the future hold? Automotive service technicians and mechanics held about 701,000 jobs in 2012, according to the Bureau of Labor Statistics (BLS). Most worked full-time for private companies, and about 14 percent were self-employed. The bureau predicts that the number of working technicians will grow by 9 percent by 2022. For information about expectations of future earnings, visit its website (www.bls.gov).

The agency says auto service and repair will continue to be in demand. In 2013, the number of vehicles on U.S. roads reached a record-high 253 million, according to an annual study by IHS Automotive, an auto industry research firm. The study also found that due to factors such as a slow economy and the increasing quality of modern cars, the vehicles had an average age of 11.4 years.

In the future, increasing numbers of cars and light trucks on the road will mean increasing job opportunities for automotive service technicians—especially those with post-high school training.

With more and older vehicles on the road, both entry-level and experienced workers will be needed for maintenance and repair tasks. The BLS forecasts that dealerships and independent service and repair shops will have the most job openings, and that most of those jobs will go to those with formal post-high school training.

# WOMEN UNDER THE HOOD

The automotive service industry is dominated by males. According to the Bureau of Labor Statistics' Current Population Survey in 2013, out of a total of 863,000 automotive service technicians/mechanics, only 11,000 were women—fewer than 2 percent. However, that is slowly changing.

Many women now work on their own cars. Others complete formal training in automotive service technician programs. With the increase in the use of high-tech diagnostics, power tools, and motor vehicle systems, physical strength is taking a back seat to analytic and problem-solving skills that women can do as well as men.

The idea of female mechanics is not new. In the 1940s—when American men went off to fight in World War II—Chrysler hired dozens of women to work on their cars. Today, however, female mechanics often face gender barriers in the workplace among coworkers and employers—but not with female customers. Many female car owners say they trust female mechanics more than males when it comes to car maintenance and repair.

As more women enter the previously male-dominated field of automotive maintenance and repair, female customers are happy to see someone they can relate to under the hood.

# What Future Mechanics Need to Know

In addition to learning the advancing technology needed for work on vehicles with sophisticated computer systems, tomorrow's automotive service technicians will need training in the science and engineering behind vehicles that use fuels other than gasoline. The price of oil and concern for the environment have spurred interest in vehicles powered by diesel fuel, hydrogen, electricity, natural gas, and the sun.

That interest also comes from the U.S. government's federal fuel economy rules known as the Corporate Average Fuel Economy (CAFE) standards, which call for an average fuel efficiency of 54.5 miles per gallon for fleets of passenger cars by 2025. The CAFE standards will influence the kinds of vehicles manufacturers build in the future. Diesel, hybrid, and electric cars have already entered the market. Others are in experimental stages.

Diesel cars have internal-combustion engines that use the same diesel fuel used by big semis and industrial vehicles. The fuel has higher energy density than gasoline, so cars and trucks that use it get more miles to the gallon. Audi, BMW, Mercedes-Benz, and Volkswagen sell diesel passenger cars and SUVs. Chevrolet/GMC, Ford, and Ram make diesel pickup trucks.

# Hybrid and Electric Vehicles

Hybrid vehicles use more than one kind of fuel. Today's gasoline-electric hybrids have traditional internal-combustion engines and a fuel tank for gasoline, along with one or more electric motors and a battery pack. A hybrid diesel and electric vehicle is possible, but the cost of manufacturing one is too high for today's market.

Many of these hybrids save fuel by shutting off the engine when the car stops. The main fuel source is gasoline, but these vehicles can use only the electric motor for short distances. The battery pack stores energy from the braking system as the car slows down or stops. The electric motor assists the gasoline engine when the car speeds up.

Plug-in hybrids use rechargeable batteries that plug into a wall socket. The first plug-in hybrid on the market, the Chevrolet Volt, was first sold

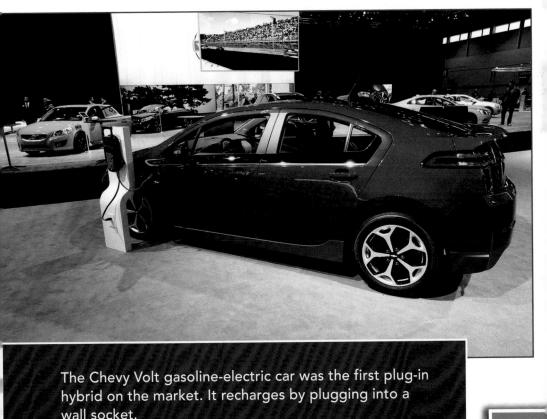

The Chevy Volt gasoline-electric car was the first plug-in hybrid on the market. It recharges by plugging into a wall socket.

to consumers in late 2010. Today, others include the Ford Fusion Energi and plug-in versions of the popular Toyota Prius and Honda Accord.

A plug-in hybrid uses the electric motor for long distances with only a little or no help from the gasoline engine. The gasoline engine provides extra power for speeding up, passing, and merging in traffic. It also helps recharge the battery aboard the vehicle. The Volt can operate as a pure electric vehicle until the battery runs low. At that point, the gasoline engine kicks in and powers the electric motor until it can be plugged in and recharged.

In electric cars (EVs), an electric motor replaces a gasoline engine. The car gets its energy from rechargeable batteries that typically must be plugged in every night. EVs come in a wide variety of sizes, body styles, and prices. Examples include the Mitsubishi i-MiEV, Tesla Model S, Ford Focus BEV, Nissan Leaf, and Honda Fit EV.

## Riding on Air?

Two other types of hybrid cars are in development at PSA Peugeot Citroën, a French vehicle manufacturer. They use compressed air to store energy. The Citroën C3 and Peugeot 208 are powered by gas engines combined with a hydraulic motor. Hydraulic systems involve moving liquid in a confined space under pressure.

When the cars slow down, energy from the wheels drives a pump that pushes hydraulic fluid into a storage unit that holds nitrogen gas. The movement compresses the nitrogen. When the cars accelerate, the pressurized nitrogen pushes the hydraulic fluid to drive the hydraulic motor. At highway speeds, the gasoline engine provides most of the power. At speeds slower than forty-three miles per hour (sixty-nine kilometers per hour), hydraulics power the wheels. The cars are expected to be introduced for sale in 2016.

# Space-Age Vehicles

A hydrogen fuel cell electric vehicle (FCEV) has an electric motor and battery along with a hydrogen storage tank. Hydrogen and the outside air mix together in a fuel cell stack. The hydrogen chemically reacts with the oxygen in the air to generate heat and water. The heat—as electricity—goes to the motor and battery. The water is expelled. For safety, the car has sensors that stop the release of hydrogen if the car is involved in a collision.

The first fuel cells were created in the 1840s and first used by the National Aeronautics and Space Administration (NASA) in the Gemini and Apollo spacecraft in the 1960s. While NASA was developing fuel cells for outer space, auto companies started working with them for vehicles. More than fifty years later, the first hydrogen-fueled electric cars and light trucks are ready for mass production.

Hyundai Motor Company, a Korean company with factories in the United States, offered the first Hyundai ix35 Tucsons in dealerships in California in 2014. Hyundai USA also introduced a new service policy. When it's time for maintenance, Hyundai technicians go out and perform the tasks right in the customer's driveway. So, some technicians already have to take the "show on the road" and be able to use diagnostic and repair tools and equipment

The Hyundai Tucson Fuel Cell Electric Vehicle (FCEV) was the first mass-produced fuel cell vehicle offered in the U.S. market.

that are easy to transport. Other FCEVs include the Honda FCX Clarity fuel-cell sedan and the Toyota FCV. More makes and models are slated for the 2017 model year.

Hydrogen-powered cars and trucks are considered zero-emission vehicles (ZEVs), a designation originated by the California Air Resources Board. The fuel-cell vehicles do emit water or water vapor, but ZEV refers only to greenhouse gas pollutants from a vehicle's tailpipe. Another ZEV is Toyota's RAV4 EV, an all-electric SUV updated from an original 1997 model. The RAV4 EV sold in California as early as 2014. Indian manufacturer Mehinda REVA sells all-electric cars in India, Europe, Japan, Australia, and Costa Rica.

Compressed natural gas powers cars and light trucks in both natural-gas-only engines and hybrid vehicles that also use gasoline. The natural gas cars work the same way as gasoline-fueled cars. The bi-fuel versions have two separate fueling systems that let them run on either natural gas or gasoline. Qualified mechanics can convert some gasoline-only cars to dual-fuel vehicles. For example, the Ford F250 and 350 super duty trucks can be converted to use both fuels. This ability offers more job opportunities for automotive service technicians skilled in that technology.

Other mass-produced natural gas vehicles include the Honda Civic Natural Gas model, which uses only natural gas, and the Dodge Ram 2500 CNG, which has two separate tanks for gasoline and natural gas. The Honda has been sold to fleets and individuals in the United States since 1998. The Dodge was first available for sale in 2012.

## Let the Sun Shine

On August 31, 1955, William G. Cobb of the General Motors Corporation demonstrated the world's first solar automobile at the General Motors Powerama auto show in Chicago, Illinois. He called it a Sunmobile. It was only 15 inches (38 centimeters) long. Since then no mass-produced solar-powered vehicles have been sold anywhere. But design teams have annually raced solar inventions for twenty years in competitions such as the American Solar Challenge road races and the Formula Sun Grand Prix, which is held on a track.

In 2014, however, Ford unveiled its C-MAX Solar Energi Car at the International Consumer Electronics Show in Las Vegas,

Nevada. It's a plug-in hybrid powered by the sun instead of the electric company. A device that acts like a magnifying glass concentrates the sun's rays in solar panels on the car's roof. The electricity from the solar panels recharges the battery. The car is not yet in mass production.

Cars of the future are here today. Some are already on the road in communities across the country and around the world. Others are on their

The Ford C Max Solar Energi concept car was displayed at the 2014 International Consumer Electronics Show. The sun's energy is concentrated in panels on the car's roof.

way to market. The world of automotive maintenance and repair is changing, too. Tomorrow's automotive technicians will need to keep up with technological advances in both mechanics and computers. If you like to work with your hands and enjoy learning new things, you can use your skills to help members of your community keep their motor vehicles running safely and well. A career as an automotive service technician may be right for you.

**BRAKE ROTOR** A disc (as in "disc brakes") that brake pads push against to stop a car's wheels from spinning.

**COMEBACK** A customer who returns with a car that was not properly repaired.

**COMMISSION** A fee based on a percentage of money the employer receives from a customer.

**CORPORATE AVERAGE FUEL ECONOMY (CAFE) STANDARDS** Federal rules that set future gas mileage goals at nearly twice today's average fuel efficiency for fleets of passenger cars.

**DEXTERITY** The ability to work with one's hands.

**EMISSION** The chemical quality of the gases released as waste products of the engine.

**FACTORY WARRANTY** A written guarantee issued to a car buyer by the manufacturer that promises to repair or replace it if necessary within a specified period of time.

**FRANCHISE** The right to market a company's products or services in a specific territory.

**GEAR** A set of toothed wheels that work together to change the relationship between the speed of a car's engine and the speed of the car's tires.

**HYBRID CAR** A motor vehicle that uses more than one kind of fuel. Today's hybrids have traditional internal-combustion engines and fuel tanks for gasoline, along with one or more electric motors and battery packs.

**HYDRAULIC SYSTEM** A system that involves moving liquid in a confined space under pressure.

**INFORMATIONAL INTERVIEW** A conversation between a professional and a job candidate so that the candidate can learn more about the field and the job market.

**LABOR CONTRACT** An agreement between an employer and its employees.

**LIFT** A machine that raises a car above the floor so technicians can see and work underneath it.

**LIGHT TRUCK** A designation for vehicles with a weight up to 14,000 pounds (6,350 kg) and a payload capacity of less than 4,000 pounds (1,815 kg). Also known as a light-duty truck.

**MAINTENANCE** Tasks that keep a car or truck in good condition before something breaks. Examples include changing the oil and replacing batteries.

**MULTIMETER** An electronic instrument that tests the properties of an electrical circuit.

**PLUG-IN HYBRID** A vehicle that uses rechargeable batteries to provide the main source of energy, with the gasoline engine used for acceleration, passing, or merging, as well as recharging batteries onboard.

**RIGHT-TO-WORK LAWS** Statutes that give employees the right to work without being required to join a union. If a union has a contract with an employer, it must cover all employees, even those who are not union members.

**ROTATING TIRES** Changing the placement of each tire (often from the front to the back and from the back to the front) to ensure even wear.

**WHEEL ALIGNMENT** The position of wheels on a vehicle compared to each other and the ground. For best tire wear, the wheels should be parallel to each other and perpendicular to the ground.

Automotive Industries Association of Canada (AIA)
1272 Wellington Street West
Ottawa, ON K1Y 3A7
Canada
(800) 808-2920
Website: http://www.aiacanada.com/index.cfm
E-mail: info@aiacanada.com
AIA is a Canadian trade association that represents
    companies that make, distribute, or install
    automotive parts, accessories, tools, and equipment.
    It works to promote the growth of the industry.

Automotive Maintenance and Repair Association
    (AMRA)
725 E. Dundee Road, Suite 206
Arlington Heights, IL 60004
(847) 947-2650
Website: http://www.amra.org
AMRA is a nonprofit trade association that creates
    industry standards to strengthen the relationship
    between consumers and the automotive service
    and repair industry. It also provides consumer
    education programs.

Automotive Parts Manufacturers' Association
10 Four Seasons Place, Suite 801
Toronto, ON M9B 6H7
Canada
(416) 620-4220
Website: http://www.apma.ca
E-mail: info@apma.ca
APMA is a Canadian association that represents
    manufacturers of parts, equipment, tools,
    supplies, and services for the worldwide

automotive industry. It promotes the industry and advocates for legislation that affects its members.

Automotive Service Association (ASA)
3190 Precinct Line Road, Suite 100
Colleyville, TX 76034-7675
(800) 272-7467
Website: http://www.asashop.org
E-mail: asainfo@ASAshop.org
ASA is an organization for owners and managers of automotive service businesses. It advocates for legislation, provides management training, and provides discounts on services to mechanical, transmission, and collision shop owners.

Automotive Youth Educational Systems (AYES)
101 Blue Seal Drive, SE, Suite 101
Leesburg, VA 20175
(888) 339-2937
Website: https://www.ayes.org/home.aspx
E-mail: http://info@ayes.org
AYES is a partnership between high schools with automotive technology courses and employers such as car dealers. It seeks to develop career-ready automotive technicians and service personnel through classroom and practical skills.

National Automobile Dealers Association (NADA)
8400 Westpark Drive
McLean, VA 22102
(800) 252-6232
Website: http://www.nada.org
E-mail: help@nada.org
NADA is an organization of new car and truck dealers

that represents members to federal agencies, media, and consumers. It also conducts research, provides training programs, and offers employee benefit plans.

National Automotive Technicians Education
    Foundation (NATEF)
101 Blue Seal Drive, SE, Suite 101
Leesburg, VA 20175
(703) 669-6650
Website: www.natef.org
E-mail: webmaster@natef.org
NATEF is a national nonprofit organization seeking to improve automotive technician training programs at educational institutions.

National Institute for Automotive Service
    Excellence (ASE)
101 Blue Seal Drive, SE, Suite 101
Leesburg, VA 20175
(703) 669-6600
Website: https://www.ase.com
E-mail: contactus@ase.com
ASE is a nonprofit organization that tests and certifies automotive professionals in an effort to improve the quality of automotive repair and service.

# Websites

Because of the changing nature of Internet links, Rosen Publishing has developed an online list of websites related to the subject of this book. This site is updated regularly. Please use this link to access this list:

http://www.rosenlinks.com/CIYC/Mech

# FOR FURTHER READING

Baechtel, John. *Competition Engine Building: Advanced Engine Design and Assembly Techniques*. Northbranch, MN: CarTech, 2012.

Codling, Stuart. *The Art of the Formula 1 Race Car*. Minneapolis, MN: Motorbooks, 2014.

Delmar. *Delmar ASE Test Preparation A-1 Engine Repair*. Clifton Park, NY: Delmar Cengage Learning, 2012.

Denton, Tom. *Automotive Technician Training: Theory*. New York, NY: Routledge, 2014.

Diemer, Hugh. *Automobiles: A Practical Treatise on the Construction, Operation, and Care of Gasoline, Steam, and Electric Motor-Cars*. Charleston, SC: Nabu, 2013.

Genta, Giancarlo, Francesco Cavallino, and Luigi Filtri. *The Motor Car: Past, Present and Future*. New York, NY: Springer, 2014.

Gilles, Tim. *Automotive Engines: Diagnosis, Repair, Rebuilding*. Clifton Park, NY: Delmar Cengage Learning, 2014.

Ginger, Helen. *TechCareers: Automotive Technicians*. Waco, TX: TSTC Publishing, 2009.

Halderman, James T. *Automotive Engines*. Upper Saddle River, NJ: Prentice Hall, 2014.

Harrison, Wayne. *The Spark and the Drive*. New York, NY: St. Martin's Press, 2014.

Hole, Steve. *Build Your Own Kit Car*. Ramsbury, UK: Crowood Press UK, 2013.

Little, Jamie. *Essential Car Care for Women*. Berkeley, CA: Seal Press, 2013.

Marlowe, Christie. *Car Mechanic*. Broomall, PA: Mason Crest, 2014.

Marsico, Katie. *Auto Technician*. North Mankato, MN: Cherry Lake Publishers, 2011.

Mom, Gijs. *The Electric Vehicle*. Baltimore, MD: Johns Hopkins University Press, 2013.

Orr, Tamra. *A Career as an Auto Mechanic*. New York, NY: Rosen Publishing, 2010.

Parissien, Steven. *The Life of the Automobile*. New York, NY: Thomas Dunne Books, 2013.

Sclar, Deanna. *Auto Repair for Dummies*. Hoboken, NY: Wiley Publishing, 2008.

Siegel, Rob. *Memoirs of a Hack Mechanic*. Cambridge, MA: Bentley Publishers, 2013.

U.S. Department of the Navy. *Apprenticeship Program for MOS of Automotive Mechanic*. Seattle, WA: CreateSpace, 2013.

Vincent, Peter. *Hot Rod Garages*. Minneapolis, MN: Motorbooks, 2013.

# BIBLIOGRAPHY

Becomeopedia.com. "How to Become a Pit Crew Member." Retrieved August 22, 2014 (http://www .becomeopedia.com/how-to/become-a-pit-crew -member.php).

Boston, William. "Volkswagen Recalling Nearly 500,000 Beetles, Jettas in U.S." *Wall Street Journal*, October 17, 2014. Retrieved October 20, 2014 (http://online .wsj.com/articles/volkswagen-recalling-nearly-500 -000-beetles-jettas-in-u-s-1413556517).

Brain, Marshall. "How Diesel Engines Work." HowStuffWorks.com, 2014. Retrieved October 24, 2014 (http://auto.howstuffworks.com/diesel3.htm).

Bureau of Labor Statistics, U.S. Department of Labor. *Occupational Outlook Handbook*, 2014–15. "Automotive Service Technicians and Mechanics." 2014. Retrieved July 26, 2014 (http://www.bls.gov/ooh/installation- maintenance-and-repair/automotive-service- technicians-and-mechanics.htm).

CarParts.com. "Alignment and Balance." 2014. Retrieved October 24, 2014 (http://www.carparts. com/carcare/alignmentbalance.htm).

Deaton, Jamie Page. "How Brake Rotors Work." HowStuffWorks.com. Retrieved October 23, 2014 (http://auto.howstuffworks.com/auto-parts/brakes /brake-parts/brake-rotors.htm).

Edmunds, Dan. "What Are Hybrid Cars and How Do They Work?" Edmunds.com, October 17, 2013. Retrieved October 26, 2014 (http://www.edmunds .com/fuel-economy/what-is-a-hybrid-car-how-do -hybrids-work.html).

English, Andrew. "How It Works: The Hybrid Air Car." *Popular Mechanics*, July 23, 2013. Retrieved October 26, 2014 (http://www.popularmechanics

.com/cars/alternative-fuel/news/how-it-works-the
-hybrid-air-car-15724045).

Environmental Protection Agency. "Section 609 of
the Clean Air Act: Motor Vehicle Air Conditioning."
September 11, 2014. Retrieved October 26, 2014
(http://www.epa.gov/ozone/title6/609/index.html).

Ford AAA Student Auto Skills. "Helping to shape the
future of the automotive industry." Retrieved August
18, 2014 (https://autoskills.aaa.com/web/aaa/home).

Ford Motor Company. "Technical Career Entry
Program." Retrieved August 18, 2014 (http://www
.newfordtech.com/).

FranchiseBuy.com. "Jiffy Lube International." 2014.
Retrieved October 24, 2014.

Hirsch, Jerry. "253 Million Cars and Trucks on U.S.
Roads; Average age is 11.4 years." *Los Angeles
Times*, June 9, 2014. Retrieved October 26,
2014 (http://www.latimes.com/business/autos/
la-fi-hy-ihs-automotive-average-age-car
-20140609-story.html).

Knowles, Don. *Automotive Technician Certification
Test Preparation Manual*. Clifton Park, NY:
Thomson Learning, 2007.

Lampton, Christopher. "How Hydrogen Cars Work."
HowStuffWorks.com, April 9, 2009. Retrieved
October 26, 2014 (http://auto.howstuffworks
.com/fuel-efficiency/hybrid-technology/hydrogen
-cars.htm).

National Right to Work. "Right to Work States."
National Right to Work Legal Defense
Foundation, 2010. Retrieved October 23, 2014
(http://www.nrtw.org/).

Nice, Karim. "How Automatic Transmissions Work."
HowStuffWorks.com, 2014. Retrieved October 24,

2014 (http://auto.howstuffworks.com/automatic
-transmission.htm).

ell, John. "What's Coming: Alternative Vehicles,
2014-'17." Edmunds.com, April 24, 2014. Retrieved
October 26, 2014 (http://www.edmunds
.com/fuel-economy/whats-coming-alternative-
vehicles-2013-15.html).

1zariu, Ovidiu. "How Pit Crews Work in
Motorsport." Autoevolution, December 8, 2009.
Retrieved October 24, 2014 (http://www
.autoevolution.com/news/how-pit-crews-work-in-
motorsport-14225.html).

ith, Kenneth. "Automotive service technicians and
mechanics." Prizi.com, June 12, 2014. Retrieved
October 24, 2014 (http://prezi.com/8lzz5-zpvebr
/automotive-service-technicans-and-mechanics).

onPlus.com. "Find a Unionized Job." Retrieved
October 23, 2014 (http://www.unionplus.org/union
-jobs).

Programs. "NASCAR Tech." UTI.edu. Retrieved
August 22, 2014 (http://www.uti.edu/programs/
nascar).

ck, Angie. "West Fargo Woman Buys Auto
Repair Shop." *Prairie Business*, September
25, 2014. Retrieved October 24, 2014 (http://
www.prairiebizmag.com/event/article/
d/20979#sthash.2uCPqhwf.dpuf).

odyard, Chris. "Serious Shortage of Skilled
Auto Mechanics Looming." *USA Today*, August
30, 2012. Retrieved October 24, 2014 (http://
usatoday30.usatoday.com/money/autos/
story/2012-08-28/shortage-of-auto-mechanics
-looms/57414464/1).

# INDEX

## A

air conditioning, 8, 28, 30, 44
air pollution, 12–13
axles, 14, 28

## B

batteries, 13, 31, 58–59, 60, 61, 65
belts, 11, 22–23
  replacing, 52
  seat, 12
Boy Scouts of America, 22–23
brakes, 5, 11, 12, 15, 22–23, 28, 59
  fluid, 22–23
  pads, 13, 49–50
Bureau of Labor Statistics (BLS), 42, 54, 55

## C

certifications, 18, 28, 29, 30, 31–32, 33
circuits, 4, 21, 48
classes, 20, 21, 31
clutch, 5–6
community colleges, 21, 23, 25, 26, 31, 35
compressed air, 33, 50, 60–61
compressed natural gas, 58, 63–64
customers, 9, 10, 11, 15, 16, 17, 19, 39, 51, 52, 56

## D

dealerships, 9, 15, 25, 31, 42, 55, 61
diagnosing problems, 15–17
diesel cars, 58, 59
diesel engines, 4, 22–23, 48, 50
diesel fuel, 50, 58

## E

education, 18, 25, 26, 33, 34, 44, 53
electric cars (EVs), 58–60, 61, 63
emissions, 6, 12, 44
  tests, 12, 13
engineering, 19, 20, 23, 25, 33, 58
engines, 4, 6, 11, 2
  9, 46, 48, 50, 58–59, 60–61, 63
  coolant, 22–23
  performance, 28, 34, 48
equipment, 16, 20, 25, 27, 44, 46, 48, 51, 61, 63
exams, 26, 28, 29, 30
exhaust system, 4, 10, 12

## F

factory schools, 25, 32
filters, 13, 22–23, 52
finding a job, 35–38
  websites for, 36–37
fluid, 8, 13, 30, 60

Ford Motor Company, 25,
    26–27
franchise, 52–53
fuels, 48, 50, 58, 59, 64
    systems, 11, 12, 15, 23,
        25, 48, 64
    tank, 58–59
    uses, 22–23

**G**

gasoline stations, 9, 42
gears, 30, 46
General Educational
    Development (GED),
    18, 48
governments, 9, 42

**H**

heating, 8, 28
high school diploma, 18,
    48
horn, 11, 12
hoses, 11, 22–23
hybrid vehicles, 22–23,
    58–60, 63
hydraulic systems, 60–61
hydrogen fuel cell electric
    vehicle (FCEV), 61–62

**J**

job interview, 38, 39–40, 41

**L**

licensing, 12, 18, 30, 33
lights, 5–6, 11
    dashboard, 22–23

light trucks, 7, 20, 42, 44,
    61, 63

**M**

maintenance, 4, 9, 13, 22,
    25–26, 40, 42, 52, 55,
    56, 61, 66
    motorcycle, 21, 31
master mechanic, 4,
    28–29, 31–32, 44

**N**

National Association for
    Stock Car Auto Racing
    (NASCAR), 49, 50
noises, 15, 29, 30

**O**

oil, 8, 13, 20, 22–23, 31,
    32, 58
    changes, 52

**P**

patience, 19, 51
pit crews, 49, 50
plug-in hybrids, 59–60, 65

**R**

racing series, 49–50
recalls, 5–6, 13–15
repairs, 4, 5, 6, 8, 9, 11, 13,
    15, 16, 17, 19, 20, 21,
    25–26, 28, 29, 31, 32,
    40, 42, 44, 45, 51, 54,
    55, 56, 66

# S

safety, 11, 13, 22–23, 61
  education, 26
  feature, 4
  inspection, 11–12, 21
  laws, 12
  procedures, 10
  recalls, 15
sensors, 4, 8, 16–17, 61
service inspection, 11, 14,
  25, 49–50
skills
  competition, 26–27
  diagnostic, 13
  interview, 29
  life, 26
  needed to be a
    mechanic, 6, 18, 19,
    20, 48, 53, 66
  problem-solving, 17, 56
solar-powered vehicles,
  64–65
specialization, 44–49
steering mechanism, 12,
  28, 46
  fluid in, 22–23
suspension system, 14,
  28, 46, 49–50

# T

tires, 10, 12, 13, 31, 46
  changes, 49
  pressure, 22–23

  stores, 9, 42
tools, 18, 20, 27, 31, 33,
  44, 56, 61, 63
trainee technicians,
  32, 34
training, 6, 12, 17, 23,
  25–26, 32, 34, 40, 50,
  52–53, 55, 56, 58
  program, 28, 30
transmissions, 5–6, 22–23,
  28, 29, 50
  fluid, 22–23
  technicians, 46

# U

unions, 30, 35, 37, 38
  shops, 37, 38
U.S. Department of Labor,
  9, 22, 42

# V

vocational/technical
  schools, 23, 35

# W

warranty, 11, 15
wheels, 12, 45, 46, 48,
  60, 61
  bearings, 13, 30
windows, 12
  glass, 48
windshields, 12, 48
  washer, 22–23

## About the Author

Mary-Lane Kamberg is a professional writer specializing in nonfiction for school-age readers. She is the author of *Getting a Job in Law Enforcement, Security, and Corrections* and *A Career as an Athletic Trainer*. She has also extensively written for *Women in Business* magazine, as well as business magazines in the fields of produce, electronic transactions, veterinary medicine, and the hydroelectric industry.

## Photo Credits